THE BEST EVER BOOK OF
CONSERVATIVE JOKES

Lots and Lots of Jokes
Specially Repurposed for You-Know-Who

Other books by Mark Young

The West Australian Joke Book
How To Promote Your Business
Dr. Young's Guide to Demotivating Employees
Guide To Selling Your Home

And about 600 other books titled:

The Best Ever Book of ...... Jokes

To find out more, check out our websites at:

www.dolyttle.com, www.thebesteverbook.com

or visit

www.amazon.com

THE BEST EVER BOOK OF CONSERVATIVE JOKES

Lots and Lots of Jokes
Specially Repurposed for You-Know-Who

Dolyttle & Seamore
New York, New York

The Best Ever Book of Jokes: Lots and Lots of Jokes Specially Repurposed for You-Know-Who

Dolyttle & Seamore
New York, New York

Dolyttle & Seamore
198 Garth Road Suite 2DD
Scarsdale, NY 10583

Publisher's Cataloging-in-Publication Data

The Best Ever Book of Jokes: Lots and Lots of Jokes Specially Repurposed for You-Know-Who.

p. cm.
ISBN-13: 9781478120063
ISBN-10: 1478120061

10 9 8 7 6 5 4 3 2 1

To All Those People
Who Think They Have a Sense of Humor —But Don't

Introduction

In my world, nothing is original. While I may be the only person who believes this, it's true. I have heard almost every joke in this book at least a hundred times—the only difference is the victim—a different ethnic, racial or religious group.

I grew up in Australia where the victim was Irish. In other states and countries the victim is often Jewish, Blond, Italian, Libyan, Catholic, Mexican, Polish, Australian, Norwegian, Essex Girl, Newfie, Mother-in-Law, etc.

Just because the person being picked on varies from country to country, it doesn't mean they're a hated minority. I would argue that it means that they're loved (after all, almost everybody wants to be the center of attention). In most cases, the goal is not humiliation, because the jokes being told are not nasty—they're funny—or at least they're supposed to be.

With that said, sit down, put on your happy face and prepare to be transported back to a time when you were young and innocent, and your friends tried to put a smile on your face.

And, if you're offended, sorry, no offence is intended. Just remember that perception is everything, and the way you perceive these jokes says a lot about you.

Mark Young

Why do people take an instant dislike to Conservatives?

To save time later.

———•———

Two Conservatives were helping a friend open a new store, and decided to take a break. Since the shop wasn't due to open for a few days, the shelves were not fully set up.

One Conservative said to the other: "I bet some old fogey will walk by, put his or her face to the window, and ask what we're selling."

No sooner were the words out of his mouth, when an old woman peeked through the window and cheerfully asked: "What are you selling?"

"We're selling assholes," replied one of the Conservatives sarcastically.

Without skipping a beat, the lovely old lady said: "You must be doing well. You've only got two left."

———•———

What do you call a Conservative who practices birth control?

A humanitarian.

———•———

Why do Conservatives make great astronauts?

They took up space in school.

———•———

Two Conservatives were riding their bikes across a university campus when one said: "Where did you get such a great bike?"

The second Conservative said: "I was walking across town yesterday, minding my own business, when a beautiful woman rode up on this bike, threw it to the ground, took off all her clothes and said: "Take what you want.""

The first Conservative nodded approvingly and said: "Good choice; the clothes probably wouldn't have fit you anyway."

———•———

There was a Conservative who was late for work during the power failure because he got stuck on the escalator.

———•———

Two Conservatives in a kayak were chilly, so they lit a fire in the craft. It sank, proving once again that you can't have your kayak and heat it too.

———•———

A Conservative was staying with a friend and asked if there was anything he could do to help out.

"Sure," said the friend. "I'd really appreciate it if you could pick up a carton of milk when you're out. If they have eggs, get six."

A couple of hours later the Conservative returned with six cartons of milk.

"Why did you buy six cartons of milk?," asked the friend.

"They had eggs," replied the Conservative.

———•———

Why did the Conservative cut a hole in the carpet?

To see a floor show.

———•———

Did you hear about the Conservative who went to a mind reader?

There was no charge.

———•———

Why don't Conservatives eat pickles?

They can't get their head in the jar.

———•———

A Conservative met a fairy who said she would grant her one wish.

"I want to live forever," said the Conservative.

"Sorry," said the fairy. "I can't grant wishes like that!"

"Fine," said the Conservative. "I want to live until Congress gets its heads out of its ass!"

"Crafty bastard," said the fairy.

———

A Conservative with one ear want into a bar.

"Do you want a beer?," asked the bartender.

The Conservative: "I've got one ear."

———

Four workers were on the top floor of a high-rise building project when Steve fell off the roof and died instantly.

After the body was taken away by the ambulance, they held a meeting to decide who would tell Steve's wife that he was killed in a horrible accident.

Finally, one of the workers said: "I used to be a Conservative, so I'm pretty good at delivering bad news, I'll do it."

Two hours later, he came back carrying a case of beer.

"Where did you get the beer?," asked one of the workers.

"Steve's wife gave it to me," he said.

The worker replies: "That's unbelievable, you told the lady her husband was dead and she gave you the beer?"

"Well not exactly," said the Conservative. "When Steve's wife answered the door, I said to her: 'You must be Steve's widow.'"

She said: "No, I'm not a widow."

And I said: "I'll bet you a case of beer you are."

———•———

How did the Conservative die ice fishing?

She was run over by the Zamboni machine.

———•———

Hear about the Conservative who broke both legs ironing the curtains?

She fell out the window.

———•———

An evil genie captured a Conservative and her two friends and banished them to the desert for a week. The genie allowed each person to bring one thing.

The first friend brought a canteen so he wouldn't die of thirst.

The second friend brought an umbrella to keep the sun off.

The Conservative brought a car door, because if it got too hot she could just roll down the window!

———•———

Did you hear about the Conservative who broke an arm raking leaves?

Fell out of the tree"

———•———

A Conservative took a second job in a restaurant to earn some extra cash for the holidays. All went well until the boss said: "Please fill the salt shakers."

It took the Conservative three hours to put the salt through the hole in the top of the container.

———•———

Three Conservatives took a small plane to the wilderness in northern Canada to hunt moose over a weekend. The pilot said: "Please remember that this is a very small plane. You can only bring back one moose between you."

But of course each Conservative killed their own moose and come Sunday, they told the pilot that last year they each brought their own moose on the plane. The pilot agreed to let them take all three dead moose home.

Just after takeoff, the plane stalled and crashed. In the wreckage, one of the Conservatives woke up, looked around and said: "Where the hell are we."

"Oh, about a hundred yards east of the place where we crashed last year," replied one of the other Conservatives.

Did you hear about the Conservative who lost $50 on a baseball game?

He lost another $50 on the replay.

What do you call a Conservative on a Harley wearing a leather jacket?

A rebel without a clue.

A crooked Conservative and two other prisoners escaped from jail. They ran into the woods and all hid in the trees.

When the guard shined his flashlight up the tree, the first prisoner said "meow." The guard said: "It's just a cat."

When the guard shined his flashlight up the next tree, the prisoner said: "whooo, whooo." The guard said: "It's just an owl."

When he shined his flashlight up the third tree, the Conservative said: "Moo, moo."

———•———

How many Conservative jokes are there?

None, they're all facts.

———•———

A Conservative was asked to be the Groomsman at a friend's wedding, but had to refuse because he didn't know anything about horses.

———•———

A Conservative was being honored by his peers at an award dinner, when suddenly there was a flash of light and God appeared before the Conservative.

God, turned to the Conservative and said: "You have made a great contribution to your field and I would like to reward you for everything you've done. You have the choice of infinite wealth, boundless wisdom or utter beauty. Pick one."

Without hesitating, the Conservative said: "Wisdom."

"Done!," said God, and disappeared in a cloud of smoke and a bolt of lightning.

There was a great silence as everyone looked at the Conservative. Finally, a voice called out: "Say something wise."

The Conservative turned to the crowd and said: "I should have taken the money."

———•———

There was a Conservative who sent 10 puns to friends, hoping that at least one of the puns would make them laugh. No pun in ten did.

———•———

How do you make a Conservative laugh on Monday morning?

Tell her a joke on Friday night.

———•———

Three Conservatives driving from Boston to Disneyland.

After three days they arrived at their destination and turned around and went home after they saw the sign saying: "Disneyland left."

———•———

A Conservative was taken to the hospital after suffering a heart attack. While on the operating table, the Conservative had a near death experience. Seeing God, she asked: "Is my time up?"

God said: "No, you have another 15 years, 2 months and 8 days to live."

Upon recovery, the Conservative decided to get a face lift, liposuction and a tummy tuck.

Upon release from hospital, the Conservative crossed the street, was killed by a bus.

Arriving in heaven the Conservative screamed at God: "You said I had another 15 years? Why didn't you pull me from out of the bus's path?"

God replied: "I'm sorry, I didn't recognize you."

———·———

A Conservative was driving down I-95 when her cell phone rang. Her friend said: "Be careful, there's a car going the wrong way on I-95."

The Conservative replied: "They got it wrong, it's not one car, it's hundreds of them!"

———·———

Do you know how to save a drowning Conservative?

No?... Good!

———•———

A Conservative was walking down the street with a brown paper bag. He ran into one of his friends who asked what was in the bag. The Conservative said: "Fish."

The friend said if I can guess how many fish you have in the bag, you'll have to give me one."

The Conservative said: "I'll tell you what, if you can tell me how many fish I have, I'll give you both of them."

———•———

Why won't a shark attack a Conservative swimming in the ocean?

Professional courtesy.

———•———

A Conservative received a parrot as a gift. The parrot had a bad attitude and an even worse vocabulary. Every word out of the bird's mouth was rude, obnoxious and laced with profanity.

The Conservative tried to change the bird's attitude by saying only polite words, playing soft music and doing anything possible to "clean up" the bird's vocabulary.

Finally, the Conservative was fed up and yelled at the parrot. The parrot yelled back. The Conservative shook the parrot, and the parrot got angrier and angrier and ruder and ruder. In desperation, the Conservative grabbed the bird and put him in the freezer.

For a few minutes the parrot squawked and kicked and screamed. Then suddenly there was total quiet. Not a peep was heard for over a minute. Fearing that he'd hurt the parrot, the Conservative opened the door to the freezer.

The parrot calmly stepped out into the Conservative's arms and said: "I believe I may have offended you with my rude language and actions. I'm sincerely remorseful for my inappropriate transgressions and I fully intend to do everything I can to correct my rude and unforgivable behavior."

The Conservative was stunned at the change in the bird's attitude.

As the Conservative was about to ask the parrot why he had made such a dramatic change in his behavior, the bird spoke-up, very softly and said: "May I ask what the turkey did?"

———•———

Where can you find a good Conservative?

In the cemetery.

———•———

Did you hear about the Conservative who froze to death outside a theater?

He was waiting to see the movie "Closed for the Winter."

———•———

A Conservative went out bear hunting and spotted one in the bushes and blasted away. The Conservative investigated but couldn't find the bear. As he was about to give up, he felt tap tap on his shoulder and when he turned around saw the bear.

The bear said: "You know, it's not bear hunting season?"

The Conservative answered: "Yes, I know."

The bear took the rifle and smashed it on a rock, threw the hunter across a tree trunk, pulls his pants down and gave it to him. He then told the Conservative: "Get out of here. I don't want to see you again."

The Conservative was incensed, so he raced back to town and bought the biggest bear rifle he could find, and returned to the forest. A few minutes later, he spotted the bear and emptied his rifle. He then searched for the body, but couldn't find it.

He then felt a tap on his shoulder, and surprise, surprise, it was the bear again.

"I thought I told you not to come back," said the bear. The bear then proceeded to smash the new rifle, and again threw the Conservative to the ground and gave it to him again. "This is the last time I'm warning you. Don't come back."

The Conservative went berserk. When he got back to town, he bought a M16 and went straight back to the forest. Thinking he saw the bear in a bush, he took aim and emptied the entire M16. Still no body, until, a familiar tap on the shoulder.

"You're not in this for the hunting, are you?," asks the bear.

———•———

Friend: "Please close the window. It's cold outside."

Conservative: "If I close the window, will it get warm outside?"

———•———

Why did the Conservative die while drinking milk?

The cow fell on her.

———•———

A Conservative was worried that his wife was losing her hearing and he thought she might need a hearing aid. Not quite sure what to do, he called the family doctor to discuss the problem.

The doctor suggested a simple informal test that he could perform to test his wife's hearing loss. "Stand about 40 feet away from your wife," said the doctor, "and in a normal speaking voice ask her a question. If she doesn't respond, go to 30 feet, then 20 feet, and so on until you get a response."

That evening, the Conservative's wife was in the kitchen cooking dinner, and he was watching TV in the family room. He says to himself: "I'm about 40 feet away, let's see what happens."

In a normal tone he asks: 'Honey, what's for dinner?" No response. So the Conservative moved closer to the kitchen, about 30 feet from his wife and repeated the question. Still no response.

He then went into the dining room, where he was about 20 feet from his wife and asked the question a third time. Again no response.

He then walked up to the kitchen door, about 10 feet away from his wife and loudly repeated the question. Still nothing.

Finally he walks up to her and calmly says: "Honey, what's for dinner?"

"For the fifth time, we're having spaghetti," said the wife.

—— · ——

How do you sink a Conservative's submarine?

Knock on the hatch.

—— · ——

A Conservative from Montreal sent his photo to a lonely hearts club.

They wrote back saying they weren't that lonely.

———•———

A Conservative is at the post office buying stamps for her holiday cards.

"May I have 50 Chanukah stamps and 50 Christmas stamps?, said the Conservative."

The clerk asked: "What denomination?"

"Oh my god!," the woman exclaimed. "Has it really come to this? Give me 16 Orthodox, 22 Conservative and 12 Reform Chanukah cards, and 20 Catholic, 18 Greek Orthodox and 12 Lutheran Christmas stamps."

———•———

A Conservative was refused service in a restaurant. "We don't serve Conservatives here," said the waiter.

That's OK said the Conservative, I don't eat Conservatives."

———•———

How can you confuse a Conservative?

You can't. They're born that way.

———•———

After being married for 44 years, a Conservative took a careful look at his wife one day and said: "Darling, 44 years ago we had a cheap apartment, a junky car, slept on a sofa bed and watched a 10-inch black and white TV. But I got to sleep with a hot 21-year-old girl every night. Now I have a million dollar home, a $60,000 car, a big bed and a large-screen TV, but I'm living with a 65-year-old woman. It seems to me that you're not holding up your side of things."

The Conservative's wife replied: "No problem. If that's what you want, go for it. If you want to sleep with a 21-year-old, I'll make sure you once again get to live a cheap apartment, drive a junky car, sleep on a sofa bed and watch a 10-inch black-and-white TV!"

———•———

Did you hear about the man who wanted to be buried at sea?

His Conservative died trying to dig the grave

———•———

Why did the Conservative write TGIF on his shoes?

To remind him that Toes Go In First.

———•———

If you see a Conservative on a bicycle, why shouldn't you hit him?

He might be riding your bicycle.

———•———

A Conservative and his wife were sitting around the breakfast table one lazy Sunday morning. The Conservative turned to his wife and said: "When I die, I want you to sell all my stuff."

"Why would you want me to do that?," asked his wife.

"I figure that you'll eventually remarry, and I don't want some asshole using my stuff," replied the Conservative.

The Conservative's spouse said: "What makes you think I'd marry another asshole?"

———•———

A police officer pulled over a Conservative and asked to see his license.

The Conservative said: "I wish you would make up your mind. Yesterday when you pulled me over you took away my license—now you want me to show it to you."

———•———

Why did God make snakes just before Conservatives?

Practice.

———•———

A man walked into a bar with his alligator and asked the bartender if they served Conservatives.

"Sure do," replied the bartender.

"Great," said the man. "Give me a beer, and I'll have a Conservative for my alligator."

———•———

There was a Conservative flying in a helicopter to a town 50 miles away. Suddenly everything went black.

After they crashed the pilot said: "What happened?"

The Conservative said: "I got cold, so I turned off the fan."

———•———

Ship's captain: "Please divert your course 15 degrees to the north to avoid a collision."

Conservative: "Recommend you divert your course 15 degrees to the south to avoid a collision."

Ship's captain: "This is the captain of a US Navy ship. I say again, divert your course."

Conservative: "No. I say again, you divert your course."

Ship's captain: "This is the aircraft carrier USS Lincoln, the second largest ship in the United States Atlantic fleet. We are accompanied by three destroyers, three cruisers and numerous support vessels. I demand that you change your course 15 degrees north. That's one-five degrees north, or counter measures will be undertaken to ensure the safety of this ship."

Conservative: "I'm a Conservative on vacation with my family in a lighthouse. Your call."

———•———

What's the difference between a Conservative and a bucket of dirt?

The bucket.

———•———

A Conservative and a friend were sitting in a bar, drinking beer.

The Conservative turned to his friend and said: "I'm tired of going through life being a drain on society. Tomorrow, I'm going to go down to the college and enroll in a class that will help me make society a better place."

The next day, the Conservative goes down to the college, meets the admissions officer and enrolls in a course called Logic.

At the first class, the lecturer explains that logic helps you to figure out how the world works. To demonstrate, he calls the Conservative up to the front of the classroom.

The lecturer asks: "Do you own a weed eater?"

"Yes," replies the Conservative.

"Then logically speaking, I could reasonably conclude that you have a yard," said the lecturer.

"True," said the Conservative, "I do have a yard."

The lecturer went on. "Because you have a yard, I think that you also have a house."

"That's right," said the Conservative.

"And, because you have a house, there's also a good chance that you have a family."

"Right again," said the Conservative. "I do have a family."

"I'm not done," said the lecturer. "Because you have a family, then logically you must have a wife. And, because you have a wife, logic tells me you must be a heterosexual."

"I am a heterosexual," replied the Conservative. "I'm impressed that you were able to work out so much about me without me having to say a word—just because I own a weed eater."

A couple of weeks later, the Conservative and his friend are again drinking. He tells his friend that he's studying logic, and offers to demonstrate his new-found knowledge.

The Conservative asks his friend: "Do you own a weed eater?"

"No," replied the friend.

"Then you're gay," proclaimed the Conservative.

———•———

Did you hear about the terrorists who hijacked a plane full of Conservatives?

They threatened to release one each hour until their demands were met.

———•———

There was a Conservative who waited two hours at the side door of a movie theatre to see the stars come out.

———•———

A Conservative was watching the scuba divers jump off a boat when his friend turned to him and said: "Why do the scuba divers always fall backwards off the boats?"

The Conservative replied: "Because if they fell forwards they'd still be in the boat, wouldn't they?"

———•———

Four Conservatives were on a plane to Las Vegas for a conference when the first Conservative said: "We've all worked together for many years, but don't really know one another. I suggest we tell each other something about ourselves that nobody knows.

They look nervously at each other, but nod OK. The first Conservative says: "Since I suggested it, I'll go first. With me it's alcohol. Every so often, I go down to a bar and drink myself silly for a few days. Not only can't I remember what I did, I have to make up an excuse to explain my absence."

They all look each other nervously, but the next Conservative slowly starts: "With me, it's gambling. Periodically,

I go down to the casino and spend a couple of months salary, and then have to explain to my wife what happened. Not easy."

The third Conservative, who is really nervous, reluctantly says: "This is very difficult. With me it's women. Every so often I go down to the red light district, pick out a girl, and spend a week in the saddle. I really have problems explaining where I've been to my wife."

They all look at the fourth Conservative, waiting. He doesn't say anything. Then one of the four speaks up: "Come now, we've all told our innermost faults. It's your turn."

He looks at the others and starts hesitantly.

"Well," he says, "I'm an inveterate gossip, and I can't wait to get off this plane."

———•———

How do you confuse a Conservative?

Place three shovels against a wall and ask him to take his pick.

———•———

What is the difference between a Conservative and a pothole?

People don't run over the same pothole more than once.

———•———

A couple recently celebrated their 50th wedding anniversary and invited their three sons, all very successful Conservatives, to a dinner that was being hosted by their local community to celebrate this momentous occasion.

The first son arrived 30 minutes late and said: "Happy anniversary. Sorry I'm late, but there was a lot of traffic on the freeway and I didn't have time to get you a gift."

"Not to worry," said the father. "The important thing is that we're together today."

Son number two arrived 45 minutes late and announced: "Happy anniversary. You and mom look great. I had a last minute meeting with a client, and I only just made my plane. Sorry, but I didn't have time to shop for you."

"Don't even think about it," said the father, "we're glad you were able to come."

Five minutes later their youngest son arrived from across town and said: "Hello and happy anniversary! I'm sorry, but my boss made me work today and I was so busy packing for my vacation, I didn't have time to get you anything."

"It's fine," said the father, "at least we're all here."

After they had finished dessert, and the members of the community had dispersed, the father turned to his three Conservative children and said: "There's something your mother and I have wanted to tell you for a long time.

"When we were young, we were very poor. Despite this, we were able to send each of you to college. Throughout the years your mother and I knew that we loved each other very much, but we just never found the time to get married."

The three children gasped and son number two said: "You mean we're all bastards?"

"Yes," said the father.

"And cheap ones too."

———•———

Why did the Conservative cut a hole in his umbrella?

So he could see when it stopped raining.

———•———

Why don't they give Conservatives coffee breaks?

It takes too long to retrain them.

———•———

Two Conservatives went out one night and got very drunk. Thinking it wasn't a good idea to drive, they decided to walk. After a few minutes, one Conservative said: "I'm tired and drunk, I'm never going to make it home."

Since they had no money for a cab, they kept walking until they hit the bus terminal. The two Conservatives looked at each other and one said: "Why don't we steal a bus?"

"Good idea," said the other.

One Conservative stood guard, and the other went inside to steal a bus. After 15 minutes, the Conservative yells: "What's happening? Haven't you found a bus yet."

The other Conservative screams back: "I can't find a 52."

"No problem," replies the other. "Just grab a 75 and we'll walk from the traffic lights."

⎯⎯⎯•⎯⎯⎯

A Conservative was telling his friend why his rent had gone up. "I told the landlord that I wanted to live in a more expensive apartment, so he raised my rent."

⎯⎯⎯•⎯⎯⎯

Why do Conservatives wear slip-on shoes?

You need an IQ of at least 4 to tie a shoelace.

⎯⎯⎯•⎯⎯⎯

A Conservative was lost wandering around the desert when he came across a clothing store. Desperate for a drink, he went inside and asked the owner if he could have a glass of water.

"I'm sorry," said the store owner, "you're in the middle of the desert, I don't have any water —but I could sell you a nice tie."

"I don't need a tie," screamed the Conservative. "I need a glass of water."

Maintaining his composure, the storeowner said: "I'm sorry that I don't have any water, but over that big hill is a restaurant where you'll be able to buy food, water or any type of drink you want."

The Conservative left cursing and started walking toward the hill.

An hour later, the totally dehydrated Conservative returned. "I'd like to buy a tie please," he said.

"What made you change your mind," asked the storeowner.

"Your brother wouldn't let me into his restaurant without a tie."

A Conservative goes to his doctor and asks for the result of the tests.

"I have bad news and worse news," says the doctor.

"Oh dear, what's the bad news?," asks the Conservative.

The doctor replies: "You only have 24 hours to live."

"That's terrible," said the Conservative. "How could the news possibly get any worse?"

The doctor replies: "I've been trying to call you since yesterday!"

What's the difference between a Conservative and a gigolo?

A gigolo only screws one person at a time.

———•———

A short balding Conservative is sitting at the bar staring at his drink when a large, trouble-making biker steps up next to him, grabs his drink and gulps it down in one swig.

"Whatcha gonna do about it?," asks the biker menacingly, as the Conservative bursts into tears.

"Come on," says the biker. "I didn't think you'd cry. I can't stand to see a man crying."

"This is the worst day of my life," said the Conservative.

"I'm a complete failure. I was late to a meeting and my boss fired me. Then I went to the parking lot and discovered that my car had been stolen and that my insurance had expired. I hailed a cab, forgot my wallet on the back seat and went home. When I got there, I found my wife in bed with another guy and my dog attacked me.

"Feeling depressed, I came to this bar to work up the courage to end it all. I bought a drink, dropped the suicide capsule in it, and sat here trying to get the nerve to swallow it, when you showed up and grabbed the drink out of my hands.

"I can't even commit suicide. It's just not my day."

———•———

A Conservative walks into the bakery and buys a cherry pie.

"Would you like it cut into four pieces or eight pieces?," asked the salesgirl.

"Better make that four pieces," said the Conservative. "I'm on a diet."

———•———

A waiter comes over to a table full of Conservatives and asks, "Is anything all right?

———•———

A Conservative owned a small ranch in Montana. The Montana Department of Labor claimed he wasn't paying his employees properly and sent an agent out to interview him.

"I need a list of your employees and the documentation showing how much you pay them," demanded the agent.

"No problem," replied the Conservative. "I have a farm hand who's been with me for three years. He earns $700 a week for 40 hours, plus free room and board.

"Then there's the cook. She's worked for me for 18 months. I pay her $550 per week for 40 hours, plus free room and board.

"Then there's the half-wit," said the Conservative. "He works at least 18 hours every day, and does 90% of the work. He makes around $50 per week and pays for his own room and board. When times are good, he gets a free bottle of bourbon on Saturday night.

"I want to meet the half-wit," says the agent.

"Pleased to make your acquaintance," replied the Conservative.

———•———

What's a definition of disappointment?

A busload of Conservatives going off the edge of a cliff—with one empty seat.

———•———

One winter morning a Conservative and her husband were listening to the radio during breakfast.

The announcer came on and said: "We're expecting 8- to 10-inches of snow today. Park your car on the even-numbered side of the street, so the snowplows can get through."

Not wanting to get a ticket, the Conservative went outside and moved the car to the even-numbered side of the road.

A week later, the announcer said: "It's a miserable winter. We're expecting another 10- to 12-inches of snow today. Park your car on the odd-numbered side of the street, so the snowplows can get through."

The Conservative went out and moved her car to the odd-numbered side of the street.

The same thing happened a couple of days later when they were having breakfast, but before they could hear which side of the street to park the car, the power went out.

"What do we do now?," said the Conservative. "I have no idea where to park the car."

The husband said: "Why don't you just leave it in the garage?"

———•———

A Conservative was drinking with a few friends. After the bar closed, a drunk Conservative brought a few of his friends back to his new apartment so they could keep the party going for a couple of hours.

He took them into the living room where there was a big brass gong and a mallet.

"What's that brass gong?," one of the guests asked.

"It's not a gong, it's a talking clock," the Conservative replied.

"No way," replied his astonished friend.

"Yup," replied the drunk Conservative.

"How's it work?," the friend asked.

"Watch," the drunk Conservative replied. He picked up the mallet, gave it an ear-shattering pound and stepped back.

The three friends stood looking at one another, when all of a sudden someone on the other side of the wall screamed: "You asshole! It's 3:15 in the morning!"

———•———

What do you call a Conservative with half a brain?

Gifted.

———•———

An elderly Conservative and his wife were having dinner at another couple's house. After eating, the wives left the table and went into the kitchen to get some coffee for the men.

The two gentlemen were talking, and the Conservative said: "Last night we went to a new restaurant and it was really great. I recommend it very highly."

The other man said: "What's the name of the restaurant?"

The Conservative thought and thought and finally said: "What is the name of the flower you give to someone you love? You know, it's red and has thorns."

"You mean a rose?," asked the friend

"Yes," said the Conservative. He then yelled: "Rose, what's the name of the restaurant we went to last night?"

———•———

Why did the Conservative climb over the glass wall?

To see what was on the other side.

———•———

During a recent password audit, it was found that a Conservative was using the following password:

MickeyMinniePlutoHueyLouieDeweyDonaldGoofySacramento

When they asked the Conservative why she needed such a long password, she said she was told that it had to be eight characters long and include at least one capital.

How do you keep a Conservative busy for hours?

Write "please turn over" on both sides of a piece of paper.

How do you drive a Conservative crazy?

Give him a bag of M&Ms and tell him to alphabetize them.

A Conservative was walking to the deli along with two of his employees when he tripped over a bottle.

The Conservative picked the bottle up, rubbed the sides and a genie appeared. The genie offered each of them one wish.

"I wish I was on a beach in a tropical island," said the first employee. Immediately her wish was granted.

"I wish I was on a tour of France," said the second employee. Immediately his wish too, was granted.

It was now time for the Conservative to make his wish.

"I want my employees back in their offices right after lunch," moaned the Conservative.

———•———

What do Conservatives use for birth control?

Their personalities.

———•———

A circus owner ran an ad for a lion tamer and two people showed up. One was a Conservative and the other a blonde in her mid-twenties.

The circus owner tells them: "I'm not going to sugar coat it. This is one ferocious lion. He ate my last tamer so you guys better be good or you're history. Here's your equipment—a chair, whip and a gun. Who wants to try out first?"

The girl says: "I'll go first." She walks right past the chair, the whip and the gun and steps right into the lion's cage. The lion starts to snarl and pant and begins to charge her. About half way there, she throws open her coat revealing her beautiful naked body. The lion stops dead in his tracks, sheepishly crawls up to her and starts licking her feet and ankles. He continues to lick and kiss her entire body for several minutes and then rests his head on her feet.

The circus owner's mouth is on the floor. He says: "I've never seen a display like that in my life." He then turns to the Conservative and asks: "Can you top that?"

The Conservative replies: "No problem, just get that lion out of the way."

———•———

A Conservative was sitting in a bar having a drink and watching the 10 o'clock news. There was a story about a man on a ledge of a building preparing to jump came on. The Conservative turns to the customer next to him asked: "Do you think he'll jump?"

The customer says: "I bet he'll jump."

The Conservative says: "I bet you $20 he won't."

Just as the customer placed her money on the bar, the guy jumped off of the building, falling to his death.

The Conservative handed his $20 to the customer and said: "All's fair. Here's your money."

The customer replies: "I can't take your money. I saw the 6 o'clock news and knew he'd jump."

"So did I," said the Conservative, "but I didn't think he'd do it again."

———•———

Did you hear about the Conservative who locked his keys in his car?

He needed a coat hanger to get his family out.

Three friends went down to Mexico one night, got drunk, and woke up in jail, only to find that they were to be executed in the morning. Unfortunately, none of them could remember what they did the night before.

The first friend was strapped in the electric chair, and was asked if she had any last words.

She said: "I believe in the almighty power of God to intervene on the behalf of the innocent." The prison warden threw the switch and nothing happened.

Immediately, the prison warden begs her for forgiveness, and sets her free.

The second friend is strapped in and says: "I am a law student and I believe in the power of justice to intervene on the part of the innocent." They threw the switch again, nothing happened.

The prison warden begs her for forgiveness, and releases her.

The last one, a Conservative, is strapped in and says: "Before I became a Conservative, I was an electrician, and I can tell you right now, you're not going to electrocute anybody if you don't plug this thing in."

A Conservative was on a United flight to Australia and the flight attendant asked him if hc wanted any dinner.

"What are my choices?," asked the Conservative.

"Yes or no," replied the flight attendant.

———•———

What's the difference between a Conservative and a vulture?

Vultures wait until you're dead to rip your heart out.

———•———

The Conservative was sitting in a fine restaurant with his wife when she looked over at a nearby table and saw a man in a drunken stupor.

The Conservative said: "You've been watching that man for some time now. Do you know him?"

"Yes," replied the wife. "He's my ex-husband. He's been drinking like that since I left him seven years ago."

"That's amazing," the Conservative replies, "I didn't think anybody could celebrate for that long."

———•———

Did you hear about the lion walking through the woods eating deer droppings?

He had just eaten a Conservative and was trying to get the taste out of his mouth!

———•———

A Conservative walked into a bar and ordered martini after martini, each time removing the olives and placing them in a jar.

When the jar was filled with olives, the Conservative got up to leave.

"Excuse me," said a customer, who was puzzled over what the Conservative had done. "Why did you put all the olives from your drinks in the jar?"

The Conservative replied: "My wife just sent me out for a jar of olives!"

———•———

What do Conservatives and sperm have in common?

A sperm has one-in-3 million chance of actually becoming a human being.

———•———

Three friends were stumbling home from a bar one night and found themselves on the road which led past the old cemetery.

"Come have a look over here," said one friend. "It's Michael Rosenbaum's grave. He lived to the ripe old age of 87."

"That's nothing," said the second friend. "Here's one named Patrick Bradley, it says here that he was 95 when he died."

Just then, the Conservative yells out: "Good God, here's a guy who lived to be 145!"

"What was his name?," asks friend number two.

The Conservative stumbles, and awkwardly lights a match to see what else is written on the stone marker, and exclaims: "It's Miles, from Dallas."

———•———

How do you get a Conservative to laugh at a joke on Saturday?

Tell it to him on Wednesday.

———•———

A Conservative needed a vacation and decided that ice fishing was what he needed to relieve his tension.

After arriving at his destination a couple of days later, he started to drill, when all of a sudden he heard a loud booming voice yelling: "There's no fish down there."

He stopped, moved over a few feet and started drilling for a second time. Again, he heard the loud booming voice yelling: "There's no fish down there."

So the Conservative moved over about 50 feet and started to drill for the third time. The same loud booming voice again broke the silence and said: "There's no fish there either."

Getting nervous, the Conservative looked around, saw nobody and asked: "Who are you? God?"

"No," replied the booming voice. "I'm the ice skating arena manager."

———•———

What do you call 25 skydiving Conservatives?

Skeet.

———•———

A Conservative and his friend were both patients in a mental hospital. One day, while they were walking around the hospital's swimming pool, his friend jumped into the pool and promptly sank to the bottom.

Thinking quickly, the Conservative jumped in and pulled his friend out.

When the medical director heard about the Conservative's heroic act, he immediately ordered him released as he was considered mentally stable.

When he went to tell the Conservative the news he said: "I have good news and bad news. The good news is you're being discharged, as you were able to rationally respond to a crisis by jumping in and saving your friend's life.

"The bad news is that your friend hung himself in the bathroom with his bathrobe belt right after you saved him."

The Conservative said: "He didn't hang himself, I hung him there to dry. How soon can I go home?"

What's the difference between a dead skunk on the road and a dead Conservative on the road?

Vultures will eat the skunk.

A Conservative walks into a bar. The bartender asks: "What will you have?"

The Conservative says: "Give me three pints of beer, please."

So the bartender brings him three pints and the man proceeds to alternately sip one, then the other, then the third until they're gone. He then orders three more.

The bartender says: "I know you like them cold. You don't have to order three at a time. I can keep an eye on it, and when you're low, bring you a fresh cold one."

"You don't understand," said the Conservative. "I have two brothers, one in Dallas and one in Nevada. We made a vow to each other that every Saturday night we'd still drink together. So right now, each of my brothers has three beers, and we're drinking together."

The bartender thought that was a wonderful tradition.

Every week the man came in and ordered three beers. Then one week he came in and ordered only two. He drank them and then ordered two more.

"I know your tradition," said the bartender. "And I'd just like to let you know that I'm sorry one of your brothers died."

"My brothers are fine," said the Conservative. "I only ordered two beers because I've quit drinking."

———•———

A Conservative was working on a construction site to earn extra cash. The boss needed a wheelbarrow. A short time later the Conservative returned with two wheelbarrows, one on top of another.

The boss said: "I only wanted one."

The Conservative said: "What did you want me to do, carry it?"

———•———

A Conservative was flying to New York in a four-engine plane, when the pilot announced that one engine had failed and there would be a 30-minute delay. The pilot said there was no reason for concern as the jet had three more engines. The same announcement was made two more times.

Finally, the Conservative turned to the person in the next seat and said: "I hope the other engine doesn't fail, or we'll be up here all day."

———•———

What's the difference between a Conservative and a trampoline?

You take off your shoes before you jump on a trampoline.

———•———

A Conservative was touring Europe in a chauffeur-driven Mercedes-Benz. The Conservative asked the driver what the emblem on the front of the car was for.

The driver said it was to line up parking inspectors. Nothing else was said until they saw a parking inspector writing tickets.

The Conservative asked the driver to demonstrate the device. The driver carefully lined up the parking inspector and went straight for him—swerving at the last minute.

Suddenly there was a loud bang. "What happened?," asked the driver.

"The Conservative said: "You would have missed him if I hadn't opened the door."

———•———

An elderly Conservative is hit by a car and brought to the hospital.

The nurse asks: "Are you comfortable, sir?"

The Conservative replied: "I make a living."

———•———

A Conservative hired a plumber to do a couple of jobs around his house. When he received the bill he was angry to find he had been charged $350 an hour.

The Conservative said: "I'm a highly paid professional and I don't earn that much.

The plumber said: "Neither did I when I was a highly paid professional. "

———•———

Did you hear the sad story about the Conservative who was given a pill that was supposed to radically increase a person's IQ. When it was given to rats, they were able to run a maze with one eye closed in half the time it took the other rats to complete the course.

Needless to say, the doctors were anxious to try it out on humans. When approval was granted, they gave it to several people including a Conservative, who took it faithfully every day.

Two years later, the Conservative earned a degree in brain surgery—an all time record.

Unfortunately, the Conservative was part of the control group that had been given a placebo. There he was, dumb as ever, and stuck with an advanced medical degree. What a waste. Really sad.

———•———

A Conservative was sitting at a bar when he notices a lamp on the bookshelf. He wanders over and begins to rub it.

Out pops a genie and offers him three wishes. Immediately he says I want a glass of beer that automatically refills itself.

A glass of beer appears. The Conservative drinks it quickly, and it immediately refills itself. He does the same thing two more times.

The genie then asks what he wants for his other two wishes.

Without thinking, the Conservative says quickly: "I'll take another two of these."

———•———

Two Conservatives were driving to their new jobs in Florida, when they saw a sign which said "Clean bathrooms."

By the time they had reached Florida, they had cleaned 32 bathrooms.

———•———

A Conservative and another person applied for a part-time job waitressing to earn some extra money. Being a high-class establishment, the owner of the bar gave them both a 10 question test to determine who should get the job.

Both applicants handed in the test, and they both correctly answered the first nine questions.

The bar owner then went up to the Conservative and said: "You both got question 10 wrong, but based on the way you answered the question, I've decided to hire the other person.

"What do you mean?," said the Conservative. "How could one wrong answer be better than another wrong answer?"

"Simple," replied the bar owner. "On question 10, the other applicant wrote: 'I don't know,' and you wrote 'neither do I.'"

———•———

What is the first thing you should do if you find a Conservative buried up to his neck in cement?

Get more cement.

———•———

A young, Conservative was walking around a field in Long Island, when he came across an old lamp. He rubbed the lamp and suddenly a genie appeared before him.

"For freeing me, I will grant you one wish," said the genie.

"I wish that there was a bridge from New York to London so I don't get ripped off every time I go on vacation," said the Conservative.

"I'm sorry, but I can't do that," said the genie. "It would be too much change. Thousands of people would be put out of work.

Government revenue would be reduced dramatically. It would mess up too many people's lives."

So the Conservative thought for a second and said: "OK, then. I'm a Conservative, and I'm tired of everyone making fun of me. I wish that Conservatives were as smart, or smarter than everyone else in the world."

The genie said: "Would you like two lanes, or four?"

———•———

Three Conservatives were waiting to be interviewed for a job. The first Conservative was called into the office, and after the normal questions was told that he would have to answer a question that tested his verbal skills.

The interviewer said: "I would like you to make a sentence using the word 'sweater.'"

The Conservative said: "My mother knitted me a sweater."

"I'll get back to you," said the interviewer. "Please ask the next applicant to come in."

After the second Conservative's interview he also was asked make a sentence using the word "sweater."

The second Conservative said: "My mother knitted me a sweater."

Of course, the interviewer was suspicious, but he told the Conservative that he would get back to him.

Getting wise, the interviewer changed the question for the third Conservative. Instead of asking him to use the word "sweater," he asked him to use "fascinate."

The Conservative said: "My mother knitted me a nice sweater with 10 buttons, but I can only fasten eight."

———•———

How can you tell if a Conservative is lying?

His lips are moving.

———•———

A Conservative returned home one night when he came across a dead body on his lawn. Thinking quickly, he called 911 and reported the incident.

"Where's the body," asked the 911 operator.

"It's at the end of Eucalyptus Drive," the Conservative replied.

"Could you please spell that for me?," the operator asked.

After a long pause, the Conservative said: "How about if I drag the body over to Oak Street and you pick it up there?"

———•———

What's the difference between a Conservative and a vampire?

A vampire only sucks blood at night.

———•———

A Conservative was walking down the street with a case of beer under his arm when his friend Peter stopped him and asked what he got the case of beer for.

"I got it for my partner," replied the Conservative.

"Good trade," replied Peter.

———•———

A Conservative and two of his friends walked into a bar and ordered three beers.

Just as they were about to take a drink, three flies appeared and jumped into each glass.

The first friend pushed away the beer in disgust. The second friend scooped the fly out of the beer and started drinking as if nothing had happened.

The Conservative picked the fly out of his drink and started shaking it over his drink and began yelling: "Spit it out. Come on already, spit it out."

———•———

What's black and brown and looks good on a Conservative?

A Doberman pinscher.

———•———

What's the difference between a dead skunk on the road and a dead Conservative on the road?

Skid marks in front of the skunk.

—————

You are in a room with a mass murderer, a terrorist and a Conservative.

You have a gun with only two bullets.

What do you do?

Shoot the Conservative twice.

—————

A Conservative dies and goes to hell. The devil greets him warmly at the gates, and as they enter a long corridor, the devil explains that the Conservative must choose a room where he will spend eternity.

As they approach the first room, the door opens, and the Conservative peers in. There's an endless circle of people standing on hot coals with weights strapped to their backs.

"I don't think I want to spend eternity here," said the Conservative.

The devil then showed the Conservative the second room.

In this room, the damned walk around on broken glass listening to elevator music.

"This isn't much fun," said the Conservative. "I definitely don't want to spend any more time in this room."

In the last room, the Conservative was surprised to find the damned standing around up to their armpits in vomit drinking coffee.

"That doesn't look so bad!," said the Conservative. "I'll stay here."

"Very well," said the Devil, closing the door behind him.

"Suddenly, the room supervisor called out on his megaphone: "Alright everybody, coffee break's over. Back on your heads."

———•———

What do you call 100 Conservatives at the bottom of the ocean?

A good start.

———•———

Santa Claus, the tooth fairy, an honest Conservative and an old drunk are walking down the street together when they simultaneously spot a hundred dollar bill.

Who gets it?

The old drunk, of course. The other three are mythical creatures.

———•———

How do you save a drowning Conservative?

Throw him a rock.

———•———

A rich man who was very close to his money got together with his Conservative and two of his friends. He then announced and that he was dying and had less than a month to live.

He handed each person an envelope with $100,000 in it and asked everyone to do him a favor after he died.

"Each of these envelopes contains $100,000," said the rich man. "Since I don't want to go to the afterlife without my money, would you please throw these envelopes into my coffin after I die?"

Every one in the group agreed, and took the envelopes.

About a month later, the rich man died and the group reconvened at the funeral.

As promised, each man threw his envelope into the coffin before it was closed up.

As they were leaving, the first friend said: "I have a confession to make. My local church needed a new altar, so I took $5,000 out of the envelope and bought it."

The next friend looked at his feet and said: "Since we're coming clean, I thought it was a waste of money to bury all of the money in the coffin, so I took $30,000 out of the envelope and bought the hospital a new X-ray machine.

Both men then looked at the Conservative, expecting him to also make a confession. "You guys are crooks," said the Conservative. "I didn't take any money. I put a check in the coffin for the entire $100,000."

A Conservative rang United and asked how long it took to fly from New York to Chicago.

"Just a minute, sir," said the United reservations clerk.

"Thank you," said the Conservative and hung up.

A man walked into a bar and asked the barman if he had heard the latest Conservative joke.

"I'm warning you," said the Conservative loudly, "I'm a Conservative who's just working part-time as a Conservative to make some extra money."

"That's all right," said the man. "I'll tell it slowly."

A man hired an unemployed Conservative as his office assistant. On the first day the phone rang, and the Conservative hung up immediately.

"Who was that?," asked the boss.

"Some fool saying it was long distance from Brazil," replied the Conservative. "I told him everybody knew that."

———•———

What's the difference between a Conservative and an onion?

People cry when they cut up an onion.

———•———

How do you get a Conservative out of a tree?

Cut the rope.

———•———

Why do Conservatives always carry garbage in their pockets?

Identification.

———•———

A Conservative attended a show where a ventriloquist who fancied himself as a comedian told 20 Conservative jokes in a row.

"Look," shouted the Conservative, standing up in the audience. "I'm fed up being insulted by all these jokes. Conservatives are not as stupid as you make out."

"Sit down," said the ventriloquist. "They're only jokes. Don't tell me that Conservatives haven't got a sense of humor."

"Be quiet," said the Conservative. "I'm not talking to you. "I'm talking to the little fellow on your knee."

———•———

A man walks into a bar and says: "I hear Conservatives are a bunch of hard drinkers. I'll bet $500 to anybody who can drink 20 glasses of whisky back-to-back."

The room is quiet, and no one takes up the man's bet. One person leaves.

Thirty minutes later the person who left returns, and taps the man on the shoulder: "Is your bet still on?," asks the Conservative.

"Yes," says the man and as he asks the Conservative to line up 20 glasses of whisky. Immediately the Conservative tears into all 20 glasses, and drinks them back-to-back.

The other pub patrons cheer as the man hands over the $500 to Conservative and says: "Why did you leave the bar before, instead of taking up my challenge when I offered it?"

The Conservative said: "$500 is a lot of money, so I went to the bar down the street to see if I could do it first."

———•———

What do you call a Conservative sitting on the grass?

Fertilizer.

———•———

A priest died and went to heaven. When he got there, he found a Conservative in line in front of him at the Pearly Gates. Saint Peter came over and said to the priest: "Just a minute, I'll be right back," as he took the Conservative away to his room.

A few minutes later he returned and said to the priest: "Follow me to your new quarters."

Along the way, they passed many people in their heavenly abodes, including the Conservative's quarters.

The priest was awe-struck by the opulence and splendor of the Conservative's quarters. There were fine silks, rare foods and drinks, soft music, and attractive young women to serve him for eternity.

The priest finally arrived at his new quarters—a small 6-foot by 9-foot room with bare walls, a plain bed and a Bible for entertainment. The priest said: "I don't want to sound ungrateful, but how come the Conservative gets a magnificent room and I get this dump."

Saint Peter smiled and said: "We have a lot of priests here in heaven, but only one Conservative."

———•———

Did you hear about the Conservative who spent four days in Macy's looking for wheels for a miscarriage?

———•———

A Conservative and his friend were repairing a barn roof, when suddenly a strong wind blew and knocked their ladder down. Since there was no help nearby, both men decided to jump.

Looking around for something that would break their fall, they saw a pile of manure. The Conservative jumped first.

"Are you alright?," asked his friend.

"How deep is it?"

The Conservative answers: "I'm fine. It's only up to my knees."

"Great. Here I come," yelled the friend as he lands in a pile of manure up to his neck.

You said it was only up to your knees," cried the friend.

"It did only come up to my knees," said the Conservative. "I jumped head first."

———•———

Hear the one about the deaf Conservative?

Neither did he.

———•———

One day a Conservative was sitting on a beach when he saw a young woman swimming far out to sea. As he watched, he saw a shark circling her. Immediately, he jumped into the water, karate chopped the shark, killed it instantly, and helped the young woman swim to the beach.

After he got back to the beach, a journalist ran up to him and said: "That was the most courageous thing I've ever seen. I'm going to let the world know about this. You'll be famous. I can see the headline now: 'Man Saves Girl From Killer Shark.'"

"What do you do for a living?"

"I'm a Conservative," replied the man of the moment.

"Great," said the journalist. "You'll see the story in tomorrow's paper."

The next day, the Conservative bought the paper and the headline read: "Conservative Kills Girl's Pet."

———•———

A young Conservative decided to turn his life over to God and thought that the best way to do this was to become a monk, so he checked himself into a monastery.

At his indoctrination the head monk told him that they were sworn to TOTAL silence—but every 10 years they were permitted to speak two words.

After 10 years of total silence, the head monk indicated it was now time for the former Conservative to speak his two words.

The monk said: "Bed hard," and then resumed his silent study and work.

Another 10 years passed, and the head monk again indicated it was time for him to speak his two words.

The monk said: "Food bad," and the former Conservative then resumed his silent study and work.

Thirty years after entering the monastery, it was again time for the former Conservative to speak, this time he said: "I quit."

The head monk shook his head and said: "I knew this was coming. You've done nothing but complain for the past 30 years!"

———•———

Did you hear about the Conservative who was asked to be a Jehovah's Witness?

He refused because he didn't see the accident.

———•———

A Conservative went to his doctor and said he had a serious problem because he could never remember what he said.

"When did you first notice this problem?," asked the doctor.

"What problem?," asked the Conservative.

———•———

A Conservative was jumping up and down on the floor yelling and screaming when a friend walked into the room.

"What's wrong?," asked the friend.

"Nothing, nothing at all," relied the Conservative. "I'm just so happy. I finished a jigsaw puzzle in record time."

"How long did it take you?, asked the friend."

"Six months," replied the Conservative. "On the box it said three to five years."

———•——

Not all Conservatives are bad, but it's a crying shame that the other ninety-nine percent make the rest look bad.

———•——

A drunk climbs on a bar stool in a bar and screams: "All Conservatives are thieves."

A man stands up and says: "I resent that remark."

The drunk shouts back: "Are you a Conservative?" "No," says the man "I'm a thief."

———•——

A Conservative and his wife in their 60s were visited by a fairy who granted them both a wish.

"I want to travel round the world with my darling husband," said the Conservative's wife.

Two tickets for a luxury cruise magically appeared in her hand.

A couple of minutes later the Conservative said: "Sorry, but my wish is to have a wife 30 years younger than me."

The fairy waved her wand, and suddenly he was 92.

Did you hear about the Conservatives' Rubik's cube?

It's white on all sides and it takes two seconds to solve.

A Conservative went to a pet shop and asked how many budgie birds were in stock. "We have 99 birds," replied the shop owner. "I'll take them all," said the Conservative. He went to a tailor and had 99 pockets sewn into his jacket. He then put a budgie bird in each pocket and went up to the top of the tallest building in town and jumped off.

The Conservative hit the ground with an almighty smack and lay there groaning until a person passed by and asked him what had happened. "I don't know," replied the Conservative. "But that's the last time I try budgie jumping."

Two Conservatives were walking home one night after drinking when a severed head rolled along the ground in front of them.

The first Conservative picked it up, and asked if it was their good friend Mike. "No," said the second Conservative: "Mike was taller than that."

———•———

An unemployed Conservative got a job at a sawmill. Just before lunch, he yelled: "Dave, I lost my finger."

"How did you do it?," asked Dave.

"I just touched this big spinning thing here, like thi...," replied the Conservative.

"Darn! There goes another one!," yelled the Conservative.

———•———

How do you brainwash a Conservative?

Give him an enema.

———•———

A Conservative opened her morning newspaper and was dumbfounded to read in the obituary column that her best friend Susan had died. Before she could do anything, the phone rang. It was Susan.

"Did you see my obituary in today's newspaper?," asked Susan. "It said I died!!"

"Of course I saw it," replied the Conservative. "Where are you calling from?"

What do you have when a Conservative is buried up to his neck in sand?

Not enough sand.

A Conservative was staggering home after a hard night of drinking with a bottle of wine in his back pocket when he slipped and fell badly. Struggling to his feet, the Conservative felt something wet running down his leg.

"Please, God," implored the Conservative, "let it be blood!"

A Conservative went to trial for armed robbery when the jury foreman came out and announced: "Not guilty."

"That's great," shouted the Conservative.

"Does that mean I can keep the money?," the Conservative asked the judge.

What does a Conservative say when you blow in his ear?

"Thanks for the refill!"

———·———

A Conservative phoned the maternity ward. "Quick," he said. "Send an ambulance, my wife is having a baby!"

"Tell me, is this her first baby?," the doctor asked.

"No, this is her husband Kevin," replied the Conservative.

———·———

A Conservative and his friend were catching the subway late one night when they came across a notice stating: "Dogs Must Be Carried On the Escalator."

"Great," said the Conservative to his friend. "Where am I going to find a dog at this time of night?"

———·———

Two mothers were bragging about their sons.

The first said: "My son is such a saint. He studied hard, got himself a degree, doesn't smoke, and he hasn't so much as looked at a woman in over two years."

The Conservative's mother responds: "My son is also quite a saint. He studied hard, became a Conservative and not only hasn't he not looked at a woman in more than three years, but he hasn't touched any liquor in all that time."

"My word," said the first mother. "You must be so proud."

"I am," said the Conservative's mother. "And, when he gets out of jail, I'm going to throw him a huge party."

———•———

Conservative: "My dog fell down a hole and I had to shoot it."

Friend: "Did you shoot it in the hole?"

Conservative: "No, in the head."

———•———

A Conservative, wanting to earn some money, decided to hire herself out as a handyman and started canvassing a wealthy neighborhood.

She went to the front door of the first house and asked the owner if he had any jobs for her to do.

"Well, you can paint my porch," replied the homeowner. "How much will you charge?"

The Conservative said, "How about $50?"

The homeowner agreed and told her that the paint and ladders were in the garage.

The homeowner's wife heard the conversation and asked her husband: "Does she realize that the porch goes all the way around the house?"

"She should," said the homeowner. "She was on the porch."

A short time later, the Conservative came to the door to collect her money.

"You're finished already?," the homeowner asked.

"Yes," the Conservative answered. "Since I had some paint left over, I decided to give it two coats."

Impressed, the homeowner reached in his pocket for the $50.

"And by the way," the Conservative added, "It's not a Porch, it's a Ferrari."

———•———

What do you call a Conservative with two brain cells?

Pregnant.

———•———

Two Conservatives won $5,000,000 in a lottery. While having a drink one night, the first Conservative said to the second Conservative:

"What are we going to do about the begging letters?"

The second Conservative said:

"We're going to continue sending them out?"

———•———

Hear about the Conservative who got stuck in a bear trap?

Chewed off both arms and one leg and still couldn't get away.

———•———

A broke Conservative decides to ask God for help.

"Dear Lord," he prays. "If I don't get some cash, I'm going to lose everything. Please let me win the lottery."

Lottery night comes, but the Conservative doesn't win.

He prays even harder, saying: "God, why have you forsaken me? My children are starving. Please just let me win."

Suddenly there is a blinding flash of light, and the Conservative hears God speak.

"Work with me on this," God says. "Buy a ticket."

———•———

How do you keep a Conservative happy in his old age?

Tell him jokes when he's young.

———•———

A Conservative walks into a doctor's office and tells the doctor she's broken every single bone in her body.

"That's impossible," says the doctor.

The Conservative says: "It's true. Look!" She then touches her leg with her index finger and screams: "Ouch!"

Then she touches her arm and yells: "Eeeooooow!"

Finally she touches her ribs and can barely maintain her composure as the tears start to roll down her face.

"See, I told you I broke every bone in my body," she said.

The doctor rubs his chin, then conducts a thorough examination.

"Well, Miss," he tells her, "I've got some good news and some bad news. The good news is, you haven't broken every bone in your body. The bad news is, you've broken your finger."

———•———

An executive was interviewing a Conservative for a position in his company. He wanted to find out something about her personality so he asked: "If you could have a conversation with someone, living or dead, who would it be?"

The Conservative quickly responded, "The living one."

———•———

How do you tell who the Conservative is on an oil drilling platform?

He's the one throwing bread to the helicopters.

———•———

Did you hear about the Conservative who took a roll of toilet paper to a crap game?

————•————

"So, have you figured what to buy your wife for the holidays?," asked Sam.

"I sure have," replied the Conservative.

"My wife made it easy. She said she wanted something with diamonds, so I bought her a deck of cards."

————•————

A Conservative returned home from work early one day and found his wife in bed with another man.

Upset, he grabbed his gun and pointed it at his head, which made his wife burst out laughing.

"What are you laughing at," cried the Conservative.
"You're next.

————•————

How many Conservatives does it take to screw in a light bulb?

How many can you afford?

————•————

An unemployed Conservative and his wife moved to a farm to reduce costs and work out what to do while the economy recovered. Their modest house had no running water or electricity.

Nine months after they moved, the Conservative's wife's water broke and the doctor arrived.

"What do you want me to do, doctor?," asked the Conservative.

"Hold the lantern. Here it comes," said the doctor as he held up child for all to see.

"Congratulations, you're the proud father of a ...," said the doctor.

Before he could finish his sentence, the doctor said: "Wait a minute. Hold the lantern," and the doctor delivered a beautiful baby daughter to the Conservative and his wife.

A couple of minutes later he again shouted: "Hold the lantern," and moments later held up a third baby.

"Doctor," asks the Conservative, "Do you think it's the light that's attracting them?"

A cop pulls over two Conservatives who were very, very drunk.

He says to the first: "What is your name and address?"

The Conservative replies: "I'm Mark Johnstone of no fixed address."

The cop turns to the second Conservative, and asks the same question.

"I'm David Harris, and I live in the apartment above Mark."

———•———

A drunk Conservative gets on a bus and asks the conductor how long the trip is between New York and Boston.

"About four hours, depending on traffic," said the driver.

"Okay," says the drunk. "How long is the trip between Boston and New York?"

The bus driver says to the Conservative: "It's still about four hours. Why do you think there'd be a difference?"

"Well," says the drunk Conservative: "It's only a week between Christmas and New Year, but it's a lot longer between New Year and Christmas!"

———•———

How do you save a drowning Conservative?

Take your foot off his head.

———•———

Why did the Conservative put dynamite in his trunk?

In case he needed to blow up his tires.

———•———

A Conservative and his two friends were about to go down the waterslide when a wrinkled old man steps in front of them.

"This is a magic ride," says the wrinkled old man. "You will land in whatever you shout out on the way down."

"I'm game," said the first friend and shouted "Gold," at the top of his voice as he slid down the slide. When he hit the bottom he found himself surrounded by thousands of gold coins.

The next friend shouted "Silver" at the top of her voice, and landed in more silver coinage than she knew what to do with.

The Conservative went last and, launching himself from the top of the slide shouted "weeee!"

———•———

Why do they bury Conservatives 20 feet deep after they die?

Because deep down they are really nice people.

———•———

How do you get a Conservative to climb on the roof of a bar?

Tell him drinks are on the house!

———•———

A Conservative lived with his dog for many years, and when the dog died, he went to his local parish priest and asked if services could be said for his dog.

The priest said: "No, we can't have services for a dog here, but that new church down the street that might be willing to do it."

"Thank you," said the Conservative. "Do you think $50,000 is a big enough donation?"

"Why didn't you tell me the dog was Catholic?," said the priest.

———•———

What's the difference between Conservatives and pigs?

Pigs don't turn into Conservatives when they drink.

———•———

A Conservative had just finished reading a book titled, You Can Be The Man of Your House."

He stormed into the kitchen and said to his wife: "From now on, you need to know that I am the man of this house and my word is law. You will prepare me a gourmet meal tonight, and when I'm done eating, you'll serve me a scrumptious dessert.

And, after dinner, you're going to go upstairs with me and we will have the kind of sex that I want. "Then, you're going to draw me a bath, wash my back and towel me dry and bring me my robe. Then, you'll massage my feet and hands. Then tomorrow, guess who's going to dress me and comb my hair?"

The Conservative's wife replied: "The funeral director?"

———•———

What's the difference between a Conservative and a computer?

You only have to punch information into a computer once.

———•———

Did you hear about the Conservative who studied all night for his blood test.

———•———

Why do Conservatives hate M&Ms?

They're too hard to peel.

———•———

What do you call a Conservative who scores well in
an IQ test?

A cheat.

———•———

There was a Conservative who worked hard all his life
and saved all of his money, refusing to part with any of it
except for essentials.

On his deathbed, the Conservative turned to his wife and said:
"When I die, I want you to take all my money and put it in the
casket with me so I take it to afterlife with me."

His wife faithfully promised to carry out his last wish and
agreed to put all of his money into the casket with him.

At the funeral, the service was held and just before they closed
the casket, his wife shouted: "Wait a moment, and quickly
put a metal box in the casket next to the Conservative. The
undertaker closed the casket down and rolled it away.

The wife's friend turned to her and said: "Girl, I knew you
weren't foolish enough to put all of his money in the coffin,
what was in the box?"

The Conservative's wife replied: I promised to put his money in
the casket and I can't go back on my word.

"You mean to tell say, you me you put all of his money in the
coffin?," said the friend.

"You bet I did," said the Conservative's wife. "I withdrew all his money from his bank account, put it in my checking account and wrote him a check. If he can cash it, then he can spend it."

———•———

A Conservative is someone who thinks the three major political parties are Republican, Democratic and Cocktail.

———•———

A Conservative walks into the bar and says to the bartender: "I'll bet you $200 I can pee into that glass on the top shelf without spilling a drop."

The Conservative contemplates this and says: "You're on."

So the Conservative drops his pants and pees all over the bar. When he's finished the only dry spot left is the top shelf.

The bar tender is beside himself with laughter, but stops laughing when he sees the Conservative laughing his head off.

"Why are you laughing?," he asks the Conservative, "You've just lost $200."

"Yes," said the Conservative. "I did lose $200, but I bet the guys outside $1,000 that I could pee all over your bar and you'd be laughing."

———•———

Why do Conservatives drive BMWs?

Because they can't spell Porsche.

———•———

A Conservative boards a plane to New York with a ticket for the economy section. She looks at the seats in economy and then looks into the front cabin at the first-class seats.

Seeing that the first-class seats are larger and more comfortable, the Conservative takes the last empty one.

The flight attendant checks her ticket and asks the Conservative to move back to her seat in economy.

The Conservative refuses.

Flustered, the flight attendant goes to the cockpit and informs the captain of the problem.

The captain goes back and tells the woman that her assigned seat is in economy.

The Conservative again refuses to move.

The captain doesn't want to cause a commotion, and so he returns to the cockpit to discuss the problem with the copilot.

The copilot says that his girlfriend is a Conservative, and that he can take care of the problem.

He then goes back and briefly whispers something in the Conservative's ear.

She immediately gets up, says: "Thank you so much," hugs the copilot, and rushes back to her seat in economy.

The pilot and flight attendant, who were watching with rapt attention, together ask the copilot what he had said to the Conservative.

He replies, "I just told her that the first class section wasn't going to New York."

———•———

What do you call a fly in a Conservative's head?

Space invader.

———•———

A man gets a call from his Conservative friend.

"I've got a problem," says the Conservative.

"What's the matter?," asks the friend.

"Well, I've bought this jigsaw puzzle, but it's too hard. None of the pieces fit together and I can't find any edges," said the Conservative.

"What's the picture of?," asks the friend.

"It's of a big rooster," replies the Conservative.

"All right," says the friend. "I'll come over and have a look."

As he gets to the Conservative's house, he goes into the kitchen and finds the pieces on the kitchen table.

The friend looks at the jigsaw and then turns to the Conservative and says: "For Pete's sake—put the cornflakes back in the box."

———•———

Why do Conservatives' lunchboxes have clear lids?

So they can tell if it's morning or afternoon.

———•———

A Conservative goes to Australia for a vacation. There he meets an Aussie farmer and gets talking.

The Aussie shows off his wheat field and the Conservative says: "Oh! We have wheat fields that are twice as large."

Then they walk around the farm and the Aussie shows off his herd of cattle.

The Conservative immediately says: "We have longhorns that are at least twice as large as your cows."

The conversation has almost died when the Conservative sees a herd of kangaroos hopping through the field.

The Conservative asks: "And what are those?"

The Aussie gives the Conservative an incredulous look and asks: "Don't you have any grasshoppers where you come from?"

———•———

What's the difference between yoghurt and a Conservative?

Yoghurt has a little culture.

———•———

What's a Conservative's idea of safe sex?

Locking the car doors.

———•———

Did you hear about the Conservative who saw a notice reading: "Man wanted for Robbery and Murder?"

He went in and applied for the job.

———•———

One night a police officer saw a Conservative looking for something under a street light. He asked him if he had lost something there.

The Conservative said: "I lost my keys in the alley."

"Why are you looking under the light," asked the police officer.

The Conservative responded: "It's a lot easier to look over here."

———•———

The circus owner puts an ad in the newspaper for a part-time, trainee lion tamer.

A Conservative thinks it's an easy way to make some extra money, so he applies and gets the job.

"What do I do?," asks the Conservative.

"Simply hold the chair, the lion will obey," said the circus owner.

"And what should I do if the lion doesn't obey?," asked the Conservative.

"Crack the whip," said the circus owner."

"And if that doesn't work?," asked the Conservative.

"You have a revolver. Shoot it into the air," said the circus owner."

"And if that doesn't work, what do I do then?," asked the Conservative.

"Well then, throw shit at the lion," said the circus owner who was growing tired on this line of questioning."

"Where do I get that from?," asked the Conservative.

"Trust me on that," said the circus owner. "You'll have plenty!"

———•———

Have you heard about the Conservative who cheated Amtrak?

He bought a round-trip ticket to Washington and didn't go back.

———•———

An out-of-work Conservative was given the job of painting the lines down the middle of a highway. On his first day, he painted six miles; the next day three miles; the following day less than a mile.

The boss came up to him and said: "Your productivity is dropping rapidly. If you don't pick up your game, I'm going to have to let you go."

The Conservative replied: "I just can't do any better. Each day I keep getting farther away from the paint can."

———•———

What's the difference between a puppy and Conservative?

If you put a puppy in a room by itself for an hour, it'll eventually stop whining.

———•———

A man died and was taken to his place of eternal torment by the devil. As he passed sulfurous pits and shrieking sinners, he saw a man he recognized as his Conservative snuggling up to a beautiful woman.

"That's unfair!," he cried. "I have to roast for all eternity, and my Conservative gets to spend his afterlife with a beautiful woman."

"Shut up!," barked the devil, jabbing him with his pitchfork. "Who are you to question that woman's punishment?"

———•———

What's wrong with Conservative jokes?

Conservatives don't think they're funny, and nobody else thinks they're jokes.

———•———

What is the difference between a catfish and a Conservative?

One is a scum sucking bottom dweller and the other is a fish.

———•———

Two Conservatives went into a bar and ordered two drinks. They pulled out their lunch from their briefcases and started to eat.

The waiter became quite concerned and marched over and said: "You can't eat your own sandwiches in here!"

The Conservatives looked at each other, shrugged their shoulders and then exchanged sandwiches.

—·—

Why is it good to have a Conservative as a passenger?

Because you can park in the handicapped zone.

—·—

"If there are any idiots in the room, will they please stand up," said the Conservative giving a lecture.

After a long silence, one attendee rose to his feet.

"Now," asked the Conservative. "Why do you consider yourself an idiot?"

"Well, actually I don't," replied the attendee. "But I hate seeing you standing up here all by yourself."

—·—

What do UFOs and smart Conservatives have in common?

You hear about them all the time but you never see one.

—·—

How can you tell if a Conservative made the chocolate chip cookies?

There are M&Ms shells on the floor.

———•———

A successful Conservative parked his brand new Porsche in front of the office to show it off to his colleagues. As he got out, a truck came along too close to the curb and completely tore off the driver's side.

The Conservative immediately called 911 and in less than 5 minutes the law arrived. Before the police officer could ask any questions, the Conservative started screaming about how his brand-new car would never be the same again.

After the Conservative had finished his rant, the police officer shook his head in disbelief.

"I can't believe how materialistic you Conservatives are," he said. "You're so focused on your possessions you don't notice anything else."

"How can you say that?," asked the Conservative.

The police officer replied: "Haven't you noticed that your left arm is missing from your elbow down? It was torn off when the truck hit you."

The Conservative looked down in absolute horror and screamed: "Where's my Rolex?"

———•———

Then there was a female Conservative who went swimming off the coast of Hawaii because she heard they were man-eating sharks.

―――――・――――

Did you hear about the Conservative who wore a glove on one hand?

The forecaster said: "Tomorrow may be hot, but on the other hand, it could be cold."

―――――・――――

A Conservative was on vacation and was told about a great restaurant in town, but thought it was closed because the sign in the window said: "Home Cooking."

―――――・――――

A Conservative went into a bar with burnt feet. The barman said: "How did you burn your feet?"

The Conservative said: "Cooking spaghetti."

"How on earth can you burn your feet cooking spaghetti?," asked the astonished barman.

"Easy," said the Conservative. "I just followed the instructions. They said: Pierce top of can and stand in boiling water."

―――――・――――

A Conservative went to a baseball game with a friend, but got stuck in traffic and arrived after the fifth inning. When they arrived, the score was still zero-zero.

"Oh good," said the Conservative, we haven't missed anything.

What do you call 16 Conservatives standing in a room around a beer keg?

A dope ring.

Did you hear about the two not-so-bright Conservatives who tried to make money selling watermelons?

They bought a truckload of melons for $5.00 each, and sold them for $5.00 each.

At the end of the day they sold everything they had bought, but couldn't work out why they had exactly the same amount of money as when they started.

"This isn't working," said one Conservative. "We're not making any money. What are we going to do?"

The other Conservative replied: "I guess we're going to have to get a bigger truck."

What's does a Conservative make for dinner?

Reservations.

———•———

A Conservative ordered a pizza. "Do you want it cut into four or eight slices?," asked the pizza maker.

The Conservative replied: "Better make it four, I'm not very hungry."

———•———

A Conservative went to the doctor and asked how to have a better sex life. The doctor said: "Run five miles a day."

A week later the doctor called and said: "How is your sex life?"

The Conservative said: "I don't know, I'm 35 miles from home."

———•———

Did you hear about the Conservative who wore two jackets when he painted his house?

The instructions on the can said: "Put on two coats."

———•———

Why do Conservatives laugh three times when they hear a joke?

Once when it is told, once when it is explained to them, and once when they understand it.

———•———

How do you make a Conservative's eyes light up?

Shine a flashlight in their ear.

———•———

Two Conservatives rented a boat to go fishing in their local lake. Amazed at the number of fish they caught, they decided to come back the next day to try their luck again.

The first Conservative asked: "How will we find this spot again?"

The second Conservative takes a can of spray paint, paints an X on the bottom of the boat, and says: "We'll just look for this X tomorrow."

The first Conservative said: "You idiot! How do you know we'll get the same boat?"

———•———

Did you hear about the Buddhist Conservative who refused Novocaine during a root canal? The goal: transcend dental medication.

———•———

A priest was seated next to a Conservative on a flight to Texas. After the plane took off, the Conservative ordered a gin and tonic, which was brought and placed before him.

The flight attendant then asked the preacher if he wanted a drink.

Appalled, the preacher said: "I'd rather be tied up and taken advantage of by women of ill-repute, rather than let liquor touch my lips."

The Conservative then handed his drink back to the attendant and said: "Me too, I didn't know we had a choice."

———•———

How can you tell if a Conservative has been using the computer?

There's Wite-out on the screen.

———•———

Did you hear about the Conservative who turned up at a friend's house in a wet shirt?

The label said wash and wear.

———•———

During a visit to the doctor, a Conservative asks: "How do you determine whether a person should be put in an insane asylum?"

"The doctor said: "We fill up a bathtub and offer the person a teaspoon, cup and a bucket and ask them to empty the tub."

"I understand," said the Conservative. "A normal person would use the bucket because it's bigger than the spoon or the teacup."

"No," said the doctor. "A normal person would pull the plug. Do you want a bed near the window or the door?"

How can you be sure that Santa is a Conservative?

Every house has at least one door and window and Santa still chooses to come in through the chimney.

Did you hear about the Conservative who became a loan shark?

Lent out all his money and skipped town.

Why did the Conservative cut off all his fingers?

So he could write shorthand.

Two Conservatives were adrift in a lifeboat. While rummaging through the boat's provisions the first Conservative found a rusty old lamp.

He rubs the lamp and a genie suddenly appears. "Thank you for freeing me," said the genie. "Due to the current economic situation and the cutbacks, I can only grant you one wish.

"That's OK," replied the first Conservative. "All I want you to do is turn the entire ocean into beer."

The genie clapped his hands with a deafening crash, and suddenly the entire sea became beer.

The genie disappeared, and only the gentle lapping of beer on the hull broke the stillness as the two Conservatives considered their circumstances.

"Nice going," said the second Conservative. "Now we're going to have to pee in the boat."

———•———

A Conservative checked into a room at his hotel and asked the lady at the registration desk if the porn channel in his room was disabled.

"No, it's regular porn, you sick bastard," replied the desk clerk.

———•———

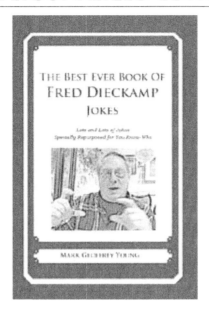

If you'd like to make this book your own, why not order a personalized copy for yourself or a friend. Simply go to www.dolyttle.com or www.thebesteverbook.com and enter your information. And we'll send you your very own copy of The Best Ever Book of YOUR NAME Jokes.

But the value doesn't end there. Not only will we put your name and picture on the cover and throughout the book, we'll also include one of your friends in the jokes so you can make fun of them.

At $19.95 per copy it's a great deal. If you're scared of the Internet, simply fill in the attached form and we'll do the rest.

ORDER! FORM

Dolyttle & Seamore
198 Garth Road Suite 2D
Scarsdale, NY 10583
212-496-8771 • info@dolyttle.com
(For faster service go to www.dolyttle.com)

Name

Address   Apt.

City   State   ZIP

Country

Email

Phone

Title: The Best Ever Book of _____Jokes

Friend's Name   _____

If you don't have a friend, don't worry about it. We'll nominate somebody be your friend, at absolutely no additional cost. Each book is $19.95 plus $3.99 shipping for the first book and $2.00 for each additional copy. Call for pricing for large orders and corporate prices.

WWW.DOLYTTLE.COM

Occupations

Account executive, Accountant, Acupuncturist, Actor, Administrative Assistant, Administrator, Aide, Air traffic controller, Ambulance officer, Analyst, Anesthesiologist, Announcer, Antique dealer, Architect, Assistant, Astronomer, Athlete, Audiologist, Auditor, Author, Baggage handler, Balloon artist, Banker, Baptist, Barber, Bartender, Beautician, Bee keeper, Benefit manager, Bill collector, Biologist, Bodybuilder, Book keeper, Boy scout, Breeder, Bricklayer, Builder, Building manager, Bus driver, Butcher, Camera operator, Camp counselor, Candy store owner, Car dealer, Caregiver, Carpenter, Carpet layer, Cartographer, Catholic, Chauffeur, Chef, Chemical engineer, Chemist, Chiropractor, Cinematographer, Civil engineer, Civil servant, Claim adjuster, Clerk, clown, Communist, Company director, Compliance officer, Computer engineer, Computer operator, Computer programmer, Conductor, Conference producer, Congressman, Conservationist, Cook, Copy editor, Courier, Criminal, Dancer, Data entry, Data entry clerk, Dealer, Debt collector, Deli owner, Delivery person, Democrat, Dental assistant, Dental hygienist, Dermatologist, Designer, Detailer, Detectives, Dispatcher, Doctor, Dog Walker, Doorman, Dressmaker, Drug dealer, Dry cleaner, Economist, Editor, Electrician, Emergency Medical Technician, Engineer, Engraver, Entertainer, Entrepreneur, Environmental engineer, Epidemiologist, Executive, Exporter, Farmer, Fencer, Fire fighter, Fisher man, Flight engineer, Food scientist, Food technologist, Fundraiser, Funeral director, Furniture maker, Garbage collector, Gardener, Geographer, Geologist, Girl scout, Golfer, Grave digger, Grocer, Guard, Guide, Hairdresser, Handyman, Hardware store owner, Hat maker, Hiring manager, Historian, Horticulturist, Host, Hostess, HR manager, Importer, Industrial engineer, Information system manager, Inspector, Instructor, Insurance agent, Interpreter, Janitor, Jew, Jeweler, Journalist, Judge, Laborer, Landscaper, Laundry assistant, Law clerk, Lawyer, Librarian, Life guard, Locksmith, Machinist, Magician, Mail sorter, Makeup artist, Manager, Managing director, Manicurist, Marketing manager, Marriage counselor, Mathematician, Meat slicer, Medical assistant, Messenger, Meter reader, Meteorologist, Midwife, Miner, Minister, Model, Motor cycle, Muslim, Naturopath, Norman, Nuclear engineer, Nurse, Nursing aide, Obstetrician, Occupational ther apist, Optician, Optometrist, Orthodontist, Paralegal, Parking inspector, Party planner, Pattern maker, Payroll clerk, Performer, Personnel manager, Pest control, Pharmacist, Pharmacy aide, Philosopher, Photographer, Physician, Physical ther apist, Physicist, Pilot, Pipe layer, Pizza parlor owner, Plumber, Podiatrist, Police officer, Political scientist, Politician, Porter, Postal worker, Postmaster, Potter, PR professional, President, Priest, Printer, Prison guard, Private detectives, Producer, Professor, Programmer, Projectionist, Proofreader, Psychiatric nurse, Psychologist, Purchasing manager, Rabbi, Radiographer, Real estate agent, Receptionist, Referee, Refrigeration mechanic, Registrar, Repairman, Reporter, Republican, Rigger, Roofer, Runner, Sailor, Sales manager, Sales rep, Salesperson, Scientist, Secretary, Security guard, Senator, Sher iff, Shoe maker, Sign writer, Singer, Skier, Skin care specialist, Small business owner, Social worker, Socialist, Sociologist, Soldier, Sound technician, Speech ther apist, Spy, Statistician, Student, Superintendent, Supervisor, Surgeon, Surveillance officer, Surveyor, Swimmer, Swimming instructor, Tailor, Teaacher, Teaching assistant, Technician, Technologist, Technology writer, Telemarketer, Tennis player, Ther apist, Ticket collector, Title examiner, Tour guide, Travel agent, Truck driver, Tutor, Tire dealer, Umpire, Underwriter, Upholsterer, Urban planner, Urologist, Usher, Veterinarian, Waiter, Waitress, Web designer, Welder, Window washer, Woodworkers, Writer, Zookeeper, Zoologist..

Nationalities

Afghan, Albanian, Algerian, American, Andorran, Angolan, Anguillan, Antiguan, Barbadian, Argentine, Armenian, Australian, Austrian, Azerbaijani, Bahamian, Bahraini, Bangladeshi, Barbadian, Belarusian, Belgian, Belizean, Beninese, Bermudian, Bhutanese, Bolivian, Bosnian , Batswana, Brazilian, British, Bruneian, Bulgarian, Burkinabe, Burmese, Burundian, Cambodian, Cameroonian, Canadian, Cape Verdian, Caymanian, Central African, Chadian, Chilean, Chinese, Christmas Islander, Cocos Islander, Colombian, Comoran, Congolese, Costa Rican, Croat, Cuban, Cypriot, Czech, Dane, Djibouti, Dominica, Dutch, East Timorese, Ecuadorean, Egyptian, Emirati, Equatoguinean, Eritrean, Estonian, Ethiopian, Falkland Islander, Fijian, Filipino, Finnish, French, Gabonese, Gambian, Georgian, German, Ghanaian, Gibraltarian, Greek, Greenlander, Grenadian, Guadeloupian, Guatemalan, Guinean, Guinea-Bissauan, Guianese, Guyanese, Haitian, Herzegovinian, Honduran, Hungarian, Icelander, Indian, Indonesian, Iranian, Iraqi, Irish, Israeli, Italian, Jamaican, Japanese, Jordanian, Kazakhstani, Kenyan, Kiribati, Kittian, Kiwi, Korean, Kuwaiti, Kyrgyzstani, Laotian, Latvian, Lebanese, Liberian, Libyan, Liechtensteiner, Lithuanian, Luxembourger, Macedonian, Madagascan, Malagasy, Malawian, Malaysian, Maldivian, Malian, Maltese, Marshallese, Martinican, Mauritanian, Mauritian, Mahorais, Mexican, Micronesian, Moldovan, Monacan, Mongolian, Montserratian, Moroccan, Montenegrin, Mozambican, Myanmarese, Namibian, Nauruan, Nepalese, Netherlander, New Zealander, Nicaraguan, Niger, Nigerien, Nigerian, Norwegian, Omani, Pakistani, Palauan, Palestinian, Panamanian, Papua New Guinean, Paraguayan, Peruvian, Polish, Portuguese, Puerto Rican, Qatari, Reunionese, Romanian, Russian, Rwandan, Saint Helenian, Nevisian, Saint Lucian, Saint Vincentian, Salvadoran, Sammarinese, Sao Tomean, Saudi Arabian, Scottish, Senegalese, Serbian, Seychellois, Sierra Leonean, Singaporean, Slovak, Slovene, Solomon Islander, Somalian, Somali, South African, Spaniard, Sri Lankan, Sudan, Sudanese, Surinamer, Swazi, Swedish, Swiss, Syrian, Taiwanese, Tajik, Tanzanian, Thai, Tobagonian, Togolese, Tongan, Trinidadian, Tunisian, Turkish, Turkmen, Tuvaluan, Ugandan, Ukrainian, Uruguayan, Uzbekistani, Vanuatu, Venezuelan, Vietnamese, Virgin Islander, Welsh, Yemeni, Zambian, Zimbabwean.

Sports

Adventure, Archery, Athletics, Badminton, Baseball, Basketball, Bowling, Boxing, Canoe, Cricket, Cycling, Diving, Equestrian, Fencing, Football, Golf, Gymnastics, Handball, Hockey, Jockey, Kayak, Martial Arts, , Mountaineering, Netball, Orienteering, Ping Pong, Polo, Racing, Rowing, Rugby, Sailing, Shooting, Soccer, Softball, Surfing, Swimming, Table Tennis, Volleyball, Weightlifting, Wresting.

Religion

Atheist, Buddhist, Christian, Catholic, Protestant, Unitarian, Baptist, Jewish, Confucianist, Hare Krishna, Hindi, Muslim, Jehovah's Witness, Mormon, Rastafarian, Scientologist, Seventh-day Adventist, Sikh, Pagan, Witch.

Political Parties

Communist, Conservative, Democrat, Independent, Labour, Liberal, Libertarian, Non-Voter, Republican, Socialist, Tea Party.

Or

Write Your own

THE BEST EVER GUIDE TO _____ JOKES

_Lots and Lots of Jokes Specially Repurposed for _____

VISIT WWW.DOLYTTLE.COM TO FIND OUT MORE.

Printed in Great Britain
by Amazon

85864517R00061